Russella L. Davis

Presents

And
We
Fell
Out
Laughin'

authorHOUSE™

1663 LIBERTY DRIVE, SUITE 200
BLOOMINGTON, INDIANA 47403
(800) 839-8640
WWW.AUTHORHOUSE.COM

First published by AuthorHouse 06/02/2009

ISBN: 978-1-4259-0345-9 (sc)

Library of Congress Control Number: 2006903067

Printed in the United States of America
Bloomington, Indiana

This book is printed on acid-free paper.

To my cherished grandparents:
Great-Grandma Earline
Granny Liz
(1922-1986)
Grandma Bennie
Grandma Sola
Great-Grandma Katherine
(1912-2006)
Granddaddy Russell
Papa Herbert
(1931-2009)
Great-Granddaddy Eugene
(1912-1992)

And to all of my family... Peace and Love

*And
We
Fell
Out
Laughin'*

Contents

REflECTION

As I move forward in my life to my next beginning,
I realize the importance of looking back. Reflection,
indeed, is important in order to establish why one's path
is on its current course.

Memories are the best source of my reflection. I
remember my Great-Grandmother Earline making
homemade custard. I remember my Dad flying a kite
with me. I recall my Granddaddy Russell taking me
fishing. I remember Grandma Sola waking everyone up
at five o'clock on Sunday morning and pressing our hair
to have us ready for Sunday school. The best perspective
in reflecting comes from these purest moments.

Often, you realize in life that you are who you are because of your history, and you still became who you are in spite of your history.
My most precious memories are private, but many of my fondest and more humorous memories have now been put to paper.

Perhaps some possess that "you had to be there" quality. Others may be instantly inviting and relatable. It is my intention to ignite memories of one's own childhood, for it is through these memories that we are able to delight in our lives as an adult. Enjoy!

Notable Williams Sayings

If you took that child's brain and put it in a bird, it
would fly backwards.

—Grandma Sola

That child is crazy as a road lizard.

—Grandma Sola

Make it in this house before GOD puts his curtain down.

—Momma

It's all right to be a fool,
but don't be a damn fool.

—Granddaddy Russell

That girl is so hot, if she pissed she'd
burn a hole in the ground.

—Grandma Sola

Got up this morning and I was walking backwards.

—Granny Liz

Williams Family Photos

Great-Aunt Laydene and Grandma Sola

Great-Granny Liz, Great-Uncle James, Grandma Sola

Grandma Sola and Cousin Vera

The Williams Children and Cousins

The Williams Children and Cousin standing in their front yard in Greenfield, TN
Left to Right, Back Row: Auntie Gloria (Jean), Margie (Momma)
Left to Right, Middle Row: Aunt Elizabeth (Tina), Aunt Rosalind
Left to Right, Front Row: Cousin Tracy, Aunt
Barbara (Bobby), Uncle Russell Jr. (Buggy)

Left to Right, Top Row: Larry, Russell Jr., Rosalind, Gloria
Left to Right, Bottom Row: Margie, Elizabeth, Barbara

Left to Right: Rosalind, Barbara, Granddaddy Russell, Gloria,
Margie, Russell Jr.

Sisters Left to Right: Bobby, Tina, Margie, Peggy, Rosalind, Jean

Granny Liz and Russella at a State Final Basketball Game

Russella, Nathan Jr. (P. Joe), and Celena during Christmas in
1984 at Grandma Sola's and Granddaddy Russell's House

Left to Right, Back Row: Margie, Gloria,
Left to Right, Front Row: Grandma Sola, Barbara

15

Celena, P. Joe, Russella, Anthony Jr., Faithe, Patrick Jr.

Momma and I picking strawberries

Russella, Destinee (Baby Sister), Earlinaka (Younger Sister)

Grandma Sola with Grandkids: Patrick, P. Joe, Faithe, Celena, Russella

PaPa Herbert and Granddaddy Russell at Chene Park in Detroit, MI

Great-Uncle James, Uncle Larry, Granddaddy Russell, Momma, Earlinaka, Grandma Sola, and Destinee

Dosy-Des and Len-Len

Destinee, Russella, Kwijuan (Step-Brother), Debronski (Step-Brother), Tavosky (Step-Brother), Earlinaka, Rickey (Step-Father) and Momma

Bring me a switch.

        —Grandma Sola

Granddaddy Russell and Grandma Sola

The Dirt Road Not Taken

Sometimes I don't know if I have a true recollection of events or if they have been told so often that they have become embedded in my memory.

One Sunday afternoon, Granddaddy Russell, Grandma Sola, my mother and I were riding along an old country road to go to church. Granddaddy and Grandma were at it as usual. She was the ultimate passenger driver. She had probably only driven a car four times, but she knew her way to everywhere, according to her. He believed they were to turn down one nameless dirt road; and she thought it was another. Granddaddy Russell finally slammed on the brakes and said, "Damn it, Sola, I'm gonna make a left on this road and I don't care if it takes us straight to hell. This is the way we are going." My mother tapped him, "Okay. You can let Russella and me off right here."

That boy ain't got enough money to buy a pot to piss in
or a window to throw it out of.

—Granddaddy Russell

Granddaddy Russell and Celena

ABC ... Easy As 1-2-3

Granddaddy Russell is probably the most ornery man on Earth, but in a way, he has every right to be. He is that man who has taken several licks, but keeps on tickin'. His left hand was severed in a riding-mower accident and his index finger on his right hand is missing its top half. All that said, he still has a great sense of humor.

Granddaddy Russell used to grand-baby-sit my cousin Celena and me when we were toddlers. We spent a lot of time with him and he used to go over our ABCs and numbers with us. One day, Granddaddy Russell began playing the number game, where he raised a finger and asked, "How many fingers am I holding up?" It was Celena's turn.

Granddaddy proceeded to raise one finger after another. He extended his pinky. She said, "One." He extended his pinky and ring finger. She said, "Two." He extended his pinky, ring finger, and middle finger. She said, "Three." He extended his pinky, ring finger, middle finger, and index finger. She said, "Four." I interrupted, "No, Celena. That's three and a half." Granddaddy was too amused to be mad. He understood and he fell out laughin'.

You Know Better

My mother says I was a serious child. When asked to recall funny or off-center stories about me, she had to really search her brain. As a child, I often played basketball or tumbled across the grass. But more often than not, I had my head buried in a book, reading or writing.

Aunt Tina, Granddaddy Russell, Auntie Jean, Piggyface and Russella at Tina's Wedding

My Aunt Tina absolutely adored me as a child. As one of my mother's younger sisters, she often watched me in the morning if my parents were working. When I was only five and just starting preschool, my mother left me with my aunt Tina to wait on my preschool teacher, Mrs. Verlie. Ms. Verlie dressed very well and drove a really nice car. On this particular morning there was an old loud car, obviously needing a muffler, passing by our house and my aunt jumped up out of her deep slumber and asked, "Is that Ms. Verlie?" I replied, "Go back to sleep, Aunt Tina. You know Ms. Verlie's car doesn't sound like that." She fell out laughin'.

Notable Davis Sayings

You better think about the future.
—Daddy

Your whole generation got smoke in y'all's heads from all that mess y'all's parents smoked.
—Papa Herbert

Your eyes are always bigger than your stomach.
—Grandma Earline

I am tryin' to learn you something.
—Papa Herbert

Davis Family Photos

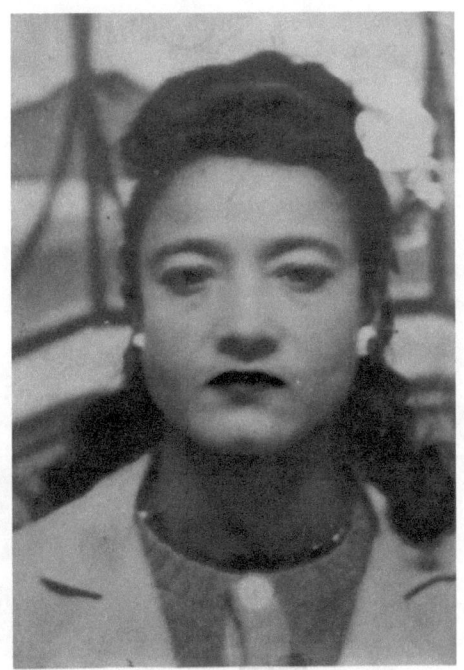

Great-Grandma Earline

Great-Grandma Katherine

PaPa Herbert and Grandma Bennie, age 18 at their prom

Great-Granddaddy Gene and Great-Grandma Earline

PaPa Herbert and Grandma Bennie with Michael (Daddy), Uncle Rodney, and Auntie Shirl in their 1st Family Portrait

PaPa Herbert, Grandma Bennie, and Michael at a Black-Tie Function

Great-Granddaddy Gene, Michael, and PaPa Herbert

Great-Great Aunt Novie, Great-Grandma Earline, Grandma Bennie
in Aunt Novie's garden in Greenfield, TN

Angeline (Older Sister), Grandma Bennie, Russella

PaPa Herbert, Russella, and Earlinaka, 4th of July in Detroit, MI

Margie and Michael at her high school senior prom

Daddy, Momma, Angeline and I at my parents 1st Home

Russella, Angeline, Daddy and Momma (who is pregnant w/ Earlinaka)

Russella and Angeline

Russella and Earlinaka

Daddy, Russella, Momma, and Earlinaka

4 Generations of Women:
Back Row, Left to Right: 4th Generation, Makeda (Younger Cousin),
Earlinaka, Russella, Angeline,
Middle Row, 3rd Generation, Auntie Shirl,
Front Row, Left to Right 1st Generation Great-Grandma Earline and 2nd
Generation Grandma Bennie

I'm a bad son of a gun and that makes you the granddaughter of a pistol.

—Papa Herbert

Papa Herbert, Korean War 1951

TV-65-GC

It has been said that once an elderly person hits a certain age, he resorts to being a child. This is true. The following is why there should be a TV rating TV-65-GC (grandchild strongly cautioned: program may not be suitable to watch with grandparents over the age of sixty-five).

My grandparents had the big TV in the living room. I only had basic cable in my room. Sometimes I would venture downstairs to watch TV with them. My Papa loved the court TV shows. He was very fond of *Divorce Court*. On this particular episode, the woman wanted a divorce. Her husband kept running around and, in her words, "having booty calls with other women." I felt myself growing uncomfortable and was making my grand escape, when my Papa asked my grandmother, "Bennie, what is a booty call?" She replied with disgust, "Herbert, don't ask me such questions." I saw my chance and hurried to leave. As I ran away, my Papa said, "Um hmm, I know you know what a booty call is." I stopped, turned around, and replied, "I know you know what it is, too."

You gonna eat your cornbread

My father never had that son he always wanted. He has three daughters, and even though I was totally into sports, the one thing I could never do for my father as a child was eat all of my food, especially my cornbread.

Daddy and I at his wedding to Momma

I used to hate cornbread as a child. I loved milk. I loved greens. I loved skins with hot sauce. But I really hated cornbread. One Sunday afternoon, everyone had finished eating and my daddy would not let me leave the dinner table until I ate my cornbread. He left the kitchen and I counted to sixty, peeked around the corner, then threw my cornbread behind the refrigerator. "Daddy, I'm done," I yelled. He walked into the kitchen and immediately looked behind the refrigerator. "How did you know? I checked to make sure you were watching the game before I did that." Daddy said, "When I was a little boy, I hated eating cornbread. I used to always throw mine behind the refrigerator, too." After that, I developed more creative ways of hiding my cornbread — such as flushing it down the toilet.

It's my car and I'll pee in it if I want to

My Great-Grandfather Eugene was so sweet. He used to give me twenty-five cents every week for making his bed, and sometimes he used to allow me to drink milk coffee in the morning with him. My father used to hate some of the things my Great-Granddaddy Gene used to let me do. But I was his little baby and loved every minute of being around him.

Great-Granddaddy Gene and Russella

My Great-Grandfather Gene lived with my family and me from the time I was five until my parents divorced. Anyone who knew my granddaddy Gene knew he liked to drink and that he liked to raise a lot of hell. He and my father used to go at it. There were so many arguments and fist-raising episodes that I truly lost count; however; one stands out vividly in my mind. My father had desperately wanted this gray charcoal-colored Cutlass. He just needed a small loan to get it. He went to Granddaddy Gene to borrow a down payment and he loaned him the money.

One evening I went with my father to pick Granddaddy up from somewhere. He was filled to the brim with his spirits, so I knew the ride was going to be entertaining. Granddaddy stumbled in and he and my father immediately started to argue. Finally, my father told him he better not pee in his brand-new car. Granddaddy Gene sobered up instantly and spat back, "I'll piss in my $500 worth."

Don't they come at the same time?

I absolutely admire my Great-Grandmother Earline. She is the quintessential grandmother. She has an amazing spirit and is truly enchanting. She used to make homemade grape juice and was the best cook ever. I baked my first cake with her. I learned the Lord's Prayer with her. I discovered I was developing breasts with her.

Great-Grandma Earline, Russella & Earlinaka
at the Detroit Zoo in Michigan

It all began when I was running around the coffee table at Grandma Earline's house. My little sister Earlinaka and I often spent a lot of time there because of our parents' work schedule. I fell and scratched myself on the left side of my chest. Because it felt as though I was bleeding, I went to the bathroom and checked for blood. As I performed my self-examination I noticed the right side of my chest was swollen. I yelled for my grandmother and she ran into the bathroom. After I showed her my chest, she simply replied, "I'll tell Margie when she comes to pick y'all up." I wondered why the right side of my chest was swollen when it was scratched on the left side, but thought nothing more of it. I was only eight.

My mother arrived and she and my grandmother spoke quietly and glanced over at me occasionally. They giggled and I just assumed they were being silly.

The next morning, instead of going to school, my mother and father took me to see the town doctor. I assured my mother that it was only a little scratch but she made me go anyway.

I felt mad and silly as I sat and showed the doctor my chest. He took a two-second glance and immediately called my parents into the examining room.

"Russella has started to develop breasts," was the first statement out of his mouth. My father stumbled and fell back into a chair. My mother rushed over to fan him and I just sat there, really confused. When my father was finally able to speak, he said, "Doc, she's only eight." The doctor told my father women start to develop breasts at all ages, some younger and some older. I happened to just be really young. Then my father asked, "Don't they come at the same time?" Fathers. What do they know about breasts?

Journal

My first journal book was called "My Diary." I wrote my first entry on October 19, 1989. It reads: *The day started off good until I went home at 1:00. I failed my eye test. I was sure I could see good. That's the story for today.*

I still keep journals. With each new journal, I open with a greeting, a sort of introduction of Russella, her desires, goals, accomplishments, and even shortcomings. I do this so I can timestamp the person I was and what I was aiming towards at that moment. Sometimes, I go back and read what I wrote in 2001 or 1993. It is amazing to have a timeline of your life at your fingertips.

What will your first journal entry read?

About the Author:

Russella L. Davis was born and raised in Greenfield, Tennessee and relocated to Detroit, Michigan at the age of fifteen where she often visited during childhood summers. She is the second oldest of four girls, and was raised by her parents, grandparents, and great-grandparents. A graduate of Howard University, this is Ms. Davis' first publishing.

www.ingramcontent.com/pod-product-compliance
Lightning Source LLC
Chambersburg PA
CBHW021255280526
45784CB00005B/2379